I0616273

The High Value Blueprint: Mastering a Growth Mindset and Self Sufficiency

Table of Contents

Invest in Yourself.. 1

Mastering the Ability to be Alone... 10

Stay on Your Purpose.. 18

Maintaining a Masculine Frame.. 26

Live Below Your Means... 34

Social Life of Abundance.. 43

Life Insurance... 53

Investing.. 59

Self-Grooming.. 67

Saving.. 75

ISBN: 979-8-218-63338-7

LCCN: 2025904791

Dedication

I dedicate this book to my boys Aaru and Ameer. I love you both.

Prologue

The purpose of this book is to give men a blueprint to success. I hope this book gives you wisdom, strength, and guidance. Implement these steps in your life and watch how your life transforms into something you never imagined.

CHAPTER 1

Invest In Yourself

"The biggest investment you can make is in yourself."

In a world that constantly pushes us to focus on things like our careers, money, and even what others think, the best investment you can make is in yourself. Investing in yourself involves more than splurging on temporary things or quick fixes. It is about making a real commitment to your long-term growth and well-being. This idea may be old, but it still lacks the attention it deserves. When you make personal growth a priority, whether it is through learning, focusing on your emotional health, or picking up new skills, you set yourself up for a life that is more successful and meaningful. This chapter explores how putting effort into yourself can be a powerful and intentional journey that can transform every area of your life, helping you reach your full potential.

The first step in investing in yourself is realizing that personal growth happens more than once. It's a continuous journey. Just like an investor spreads their money across different areas for long-term growth, you need to find different ways to invest in yourself. This could mean learning something new, improving your skills, taking care of your body, or focusing on your emotional well-being. Every small effort adds up over time, leading to a more fulfilling life. Much like compound interest, those little, consistent efforts build up and bring rewards far bigger than you might expect.

One of the best ways to invest in yourself is through education. Learning does not stop once you finish high school. In fact, the most successful people are lifelong learners. This does not mean you have to go back to school or get another degree, though that could be a good choice for some. It's about taking every chance to grow your knowledge. Books, online courses, podcasts, and webinars are all full of valuable insights waiting to be discovered. Each new piece of information you pick up adds value to your life and gives you the tools to handle the complexities of the world. Education also boosts your adaptability, helping you stay relevant as everything changes around you. When you invest in knowledge, you give yourself the ability to solve problems, innovate, and grow in ways you never expected.

However, investing in yourself involves more than just intellectual development. Personal well-being both physical and mental is another important part of self-investment. Health is wealth. Without good health, all the money, education, and achievements in the world lose their meaning. Physical health is the vessel that carries you through life, and without it, even the best plans can fall apart. Investing in your health means maintaining a balanced diet, committing to regular exercise, and making sure you get enough rest. The benefits of such investments are immediate and long-lasting. A well-maintained body supports your mental clarity and energy levels and also boosts your emotional resilience. Feeling good physically makes it easier to face life's challenges and pursue your goals with energy and enthusiasm.

Mental health is another important area of investment. It's easy to overlook emotional well-being in a world that celebrates hustle and productivity, but the truth is your mental health matters just as much, if not more, than your physical health. Practices like meditation, mindfulness, therapy, and journaling offer ways to calm the mind, process emotions, and release stress. They help you become more self-aware, which allows you to make better decisions, handle conflicts with ease, and approach life with a sense of purpose. Investing in your mental health helps you stay grounded, even in tough times, and builds a positive mindset that attracts opportunities.

Another important part of self-investment is building up your skill set. Skills are what fuel both professional and personal growth. In a world that's constantly evolving, picking up new skills is a must. Technical skills like coding, digital marketing, or data analysis are highly sought after and can lead to great financial rewards. But soft skills, like communication, leadership, and emotional intelligence, are just as valuable. Learning how to manage your time, think creatively to solve problems, and keep a growth mindset are all skills that can boost both your personal and professional life. Investing in your skills sometimes means putting in the work, staying curious, and sometimes stepping outside your comfort zone.

As you grow these abilities, you'll open up new opportunities and gain more confidence.

Equally important is investing in building and maintaining relationships. Humans are social creatures, and the connections we build influence the direction of our lives. Surrounding yourself with positive, supportive people who challenge you to grow boosts your chances of success. Networking is about creating a community of like-minded individuals who inspire, motivate, and encourage you. Strong relationships promote collaboration, which offers emotional support during tough times, and help you build the social capital necessary to succeed in today's interconnected world. Your network is an extension of yourself. Investing in genuine, authentic connections enriches your life and opens doors to greater opportunities.

Financial literacy is another powerful way to invest in yourself. While money can't buy happiness, financial independence gives you the freedom to chase your dreams without constantly worrying about making ends meet. Understanding personal finance plays a big role in building wealth and achieving financial freedom. Learning how to budget, save, invest, and reduce debt can completely change your financial future. Financial literacy helps you make better decisions about your career, life goals, and personal choices. Being smart with both your financial portfolio and your personal development makes sure you're ready for any economic challenges that come your way.

The real secret to investing in yourself is *consistency*. Just like any long-term investment plan, it takes patience and effort to see the rewards. You might not notice changes right away, but as time goes on, you'll start to see the difference in your life. The small, daily efforts you make in your education, health, skills, and relationships will gradually add up and create a positive ripple effect throughout your life. You'll feel more confident, capable, and ready to take on whatever comes your way. Plus, when you invest in yourself, you set a great example for others, whether it's your kids, coworkers, or friends, and help build a culture of growth and improvement.

In the end, investing in yourself is investing in your future. You are your most valuable asset, and it's up to you to commit to your growth and well-being. It's easy to look outside yourself for answers or rely on external things to define success, but real success starts from within. The more you invest in yourself, the more you unlock your potential, improve your life, and create the future you've always wanted. The returns on this investment are endless and will last a lifetime. Investing in yourself is more than just working toward success. It's about creating a life full of meaning, purpose, and fulfillment. The journey of self-investment is ongoing, and every step you take brings you closer to becoming the best version of yourself.

CHAPTER 2

Mastering The Ability To Be Alone

"Mastering the ability to be alone is a journey to self-discovery and peace"

In a time when we're constantly connected, being alone can often feel uncomfortable or even scary. A lot of people link solitude with loneliness, but learning how to be alone can actually bring a sense of peace, self-discovery, and personal growth. The first step is changing how we view being alone. It's not about the lack of other people but the chance to focus on ourselves. Being alone gives you the opportunity to reconnect with your own thoughts, desires, and emotions. In these quiet moments, away from the chaos of the world, we really get to understand who we are.

Learning to be alone begins with accepting the discomfort that comes when you're by yourself. It's normal to feel restless or uneasy at first, but over time, solitude becomes a place for personal exploration. Being alone is not the same as being lonely; it's about carving out space for yourself, away from the expectations, judgments, and distractions of others. This space gives you room to reflect, be creative, and grow emotionally. When you're alone, you have the freedom to understand your true desires and needs without outside pressures influencing you.

One of the first challenges in embracing solitude is breaking free from the idea that being alone means you're unworthy or inadequate. In a culture that pushes constant connectivity, it can feel like something is wrong if you enjoy or even seek time alone. But solitude should be seen as an important skill, one that helps you recharge, find clarity, and strengthen your sense of who you are. The reality is that solitude lets you connect more with yourself and the world around you. In a culture that values being busy over being present, learning how to be alone is a form of resistance. It's a way of taking back your peace and your time.

The next step in learning how to be alone is developing the inner resources that make solitude feel more refreshing than uncomfortable. Many people turn to distractions like TV, social media, or even other people to avoid their own thoughts. But being comfortable with solitude means facing those thoughts directly. It's about learning how to sit in silence and just be with yourself without rushing to fill the space with noise or activity. This might involve meditation, journaling, or simply being present in the moment. It can feel tough at first, but with time and practice, you'll get more comfortable with the silence and use it to build mindfulness.

Being alone also gives us a chance to tap into our creative side. Many artists, writers, musicians, and thinkers throughout history have said that solitude sparked some of their best work. Alone time is often when the most innovative ideas come to life. Whether it's a quiet walk in nature, deep thinking, or working on a personal project, solitude can unlock creativity in ways being around others never could. It lets you focus on your passions, hobbies, and dreams without distractions. When you're alone, you can explore your thoughts without worrying about judgment, and this freedom fuels self-expression.

Being able to spend time alone also helps build emotional resilience. When we're always surrounded by people, we can rely on external validation or support to manage our emotions. Learning to be comfortable alone helps you become better at handling your emotions on your own. This involves finding peace within yourself, even during tough times. Solitude gives us the space to reflect on our feelings, process tough emotions, and really understand ourselves. This emotional awareness helps us grow and it also makes our relationships with others stronger.

The ability to be alone also provides clarity. With everything going on in daily life, it's easy to get caught up in what others expect or think. Time alone lets you step back from all those outside influences and see things more clearly, helping you understand your own goals, values, and desires. It's in these quiet moments that we figure out what truly matters. When you're alone, you have the space to focus on your own happiness and make choices that align with who you really are. Whether it's reevaluating your career, looking at your relationships, or thinking about the kind of life you want, being alone helps you make decisions with more confidence.

Solitude has nothing to do with shutting yourself off; it's about finding balance. Being comfortable on your own also means knowing when to reach out and connect with others. It's important to remember that being alone has nothing to do with pulling away from the world. Relationships are key, and connecting with others is a big part of life. The goal is not to avoid people but to find a healthy balance between time alone and time with others. When you learn to enjoy your own company, you can engage with others more fully without needing outside validation to feel complete.

As you become more comfortable being alone, you'll start to see it as a source of strength. The more you learn to be at peace with yourself, the more confident and centered you'll feel. You'll no longer fear being alone because you'll begin to appreciate the time you spend with yourself. Solitude will no longer seem like an empty void to be avoided; instead, it will become a special space for growth, clarity, and creativity. In this space, you can fully embrace your potential, free from the distractions of the world.

Learning to be alone helps you gain a better understanding of who you are, what you need, and what makes you happy. Solitude gives you the space to recharge, tap into your inner wisdom, and find peace. It allows you to live life on your terms without the pressure of other people's expectations. Being alone is not something to fear; it's a powerful space where you can uncover the truth of who you are and create a life that truly reflects your values and desires. When embraced fully, solitude becomes more than just a practice; it's a path to self-discovery, fulfillment, and peace.

CHAPTER 3

Stay on Your Purpose

"Be intentional. Set goals and achieve them."

With so many distractions pulling us in different directions, staying focused on your purpose can be tough. We live in a culture that encourages distractions, instant gratification, and shifting goals. Still, true fulfillment comes from having a clear sense of purpose and sticking with it, no matter what the challenges. Living with purpose means aligning what you do, think, and want with what matters most to you: your values, passions, and long-

18

term goals. It's all about self-discovery, growth, and resilience. Staying on track requires understanding who you are, why you do what you do, and how to face the obstacles that come up along the way. This chapter will explore how you can develop a sense of purpose and stay focused, even when life throws you off course.

Staying on your purpose starts with really understanding what that purpose is. Many people go through life without ever stopping to ask themselves, "What is my purpose?" Without this clarity, it's easy to feel dissatisfied and lost. Finding your purpose starts with taking a moment to reflect and ask yourself what excites you, what you're passionate about, and what values matter most to you. It's about figuring out what you want to give to the world and how you can make a real difference. This can take time, and your purpose might change, but the important thing is staying connected to it. When you know your purpose, it guides everything you do.

Once you've figured out your purpose, staying focused on it takes real commitment. In our ever-changing world, it's easy to get distracted by outside pressures. The demands of others, societal expectations, and constant distractions can all pull you off course. But true fulfillment comes from staying true to your own path, not from seeking approval or validation from others. It involves saying no to things that pull you away from what matters most, even if they seem appealing or offer quick rewards. Setting boundaries and learning to prioritize what really counts is important. This means making choices that align with your long-term vision, even when it's tough.

Another important part of staying on your purpose is staying strong when things get tough. Going after your purpose often means facing challenges, setbacks, and moments of doubt. There will be times when you question if it's worth it or wonder if you should try something else. In those moments, it's important to remind yourself why you started this journey in the first place. Resilience means seeing obstacles as part of your growth. Instead of thinking of setbacks as failures, see them as chances to learn, adapt, and strengthen your determination. Every time you push through a tough moment, you get closer to reaching your purpose. Staying on track involves sticking with your vision, even when the path gets difficult.

A powerful way to stay focused on your purpose is through mindfulness. Distractions are everywhere, from social media notifications to the demands of work and family. Staying present in the moment helps you stay connected to your purpose and keeps you from being pulled away by things that don't align with your goals. Mindfulness lets you quiet the noise, tune into your inner self, and focus on what really matters. When you practice mindfulness, you become more aware of how your actions and choices line up with your purpose, making it easier to make decisions that support your goals. It takes discipline, but it can really improve your ability to stay on track.

Keeping your passion and motivation alive over time is just as important. It's easy to stay focused when things are going smoothly, but how do you keep going when the excitement fades or challenges pop up? The trick is to regularly remind yourself why you started in the first place. Think about the impact you want to make and the legacy you want to leave behind. Break your bigger goals into smaller, achievable steps, and celebrate each win along the way. Focusing on small victories helps keep your motivation high and keeps you moving forward. Also, surrounding yourself with like-minded people, whether they're mentors, friends, or a supportive community, gives you the encouragement and inspiration to stay on track.

Self-care plays a huge role in staying on your purpose, too. It might seem odd, but taking time for yourself is important for keeping your energy and focus sharp. Burnout is a real thing when you're chasing something meaningful, and without taking care of yourself, it's easy to get worn out and lose sight of your goals. Make rest, physical health, and emotional well-being a priority so you can keep going strong. Staying on your purpose means working smart, managing your energy, and knowing when to take a break to recharge.

Staying on your purpose also means being able to adapt to change. Life is unpredictable, and the road to achieving your purpose rarely follows a straight path. Unexpected events, changes in circumstances, or shifts in your desires might require you to adjust your course. The important part is staying flexible and open-minded. While your ultimate purpose may remain the same, the way you go about it might change as you learn more about yourself and the world around you. See change as a chance to grow, and be willing to shift when necessary. Staying on your purpose means not holding onto an old plan, it's about being able to adjust while staying true to your vision.

Another part of staying on your purpose is finding fulfillment in the process, not just the outcome. Having a clear goal matters, but it's just as important to appreciate the journey. If you focus only on the end result, you might miss the valuable lessons, connections, and experiences along the way. Staying on your purpose means embracing the ups and downs, celebrating the small wins, and finding meaning in each step of the journey. The pursuit of purpose itself becomes a source of joy, rather than just a way to get to a distant goal.

Keeping your focus on your purpose is an ongoing process that takes clarity, resilience, mindfulness, and adaptability. It's about consistently aligning your actions with your core values and sticking to your vision, even when life gets uncertain. Staying true to your purpose helps you build a life of intention, fulfillment, and real meaning. It's not always easy, and the journey can be tough, but the rewards of living with purpose are priceless. When you stay focused on your purpose, you find the strength to face life's challenges, and in doing so, you create a life that's truly yours, a life of authenticity, satisfaction, and impact.

CHAPTER 4

Maintaining a Masculine Frame

"Always remain in a masculine frame."

In a society that values fluidity, diverse identities, and different forms of self-expression, the idea of a "masculine frame" still holds significant importance for many men. A masculine frame focuses on building inner strength, clarity, and self-assurance. It's the base that helps a man shape his character, purpose, and ability to face life confidently. This chapter explains how to develop and maintain a masculine frame that's rooted in respect, discipline, and emotional intelligence, helping men lead themselves and others with integrity and resilience.

A masculine frame starts with self-awareness. Before a man can develop or maintain his frame, he needs to understand what it means and how it shows up in his life. It's built on a few key elements: physical presence, emotional control, living with purpose, and knowing how to set healthy boundaries. The foundation of a masculine frame is the commitment to improving yourself, mentally, physically, and emotionally. A man with a strong frame is someone who knows who he is, what he stands for, and what he's working toward. His actions line up with his values, and he doesn't bend under external pressure. He leads by example, not through force, but through consistency, authenticity, and personal strength.

For a man working to build or maintain a masculine frame, physical health is the first area to focus on. The body is how life is experienced, and if it's weak or neglected, it affects physical well-being and also mental state, energy, and the ability to assert oneself. A masculine frame starts with physical discipline, regular exercise, good nutrition, and rest. Strengthening the body through weightlifting, martial arts, or endurance sports boosts physical presence and builds resilience, determination, and focus. A man who takes care of his health radiates confidence and self-control, both key components of a masculine frame. Physical strength also supports mental and emotional fortitude, allowing a man to carry himself with poise.

Another important part of developing a masculine frame is emotional control. Emotional intelligence, especially the ability to stay calm under pressure, sets apart a man with a solid frame from one who lacks it. A strong masculine frame is not about suppressing emotions, but about handling them in a healthy way.

Men are often taught to hide their feelings, thinking vulnerability makes them weak. But true emotional strength comes from knowing and understanding emotions without letting them dictate behavior. A man who has developed his masculine frame can face adversity without being swayed by fear, anger, or frustration. He's not reactive, but intentional in his actions. He can show compassion, assertiveness, and calmness, even when challenges arise.

Purpose is another cornerstone of a masculine frame. A man without a clear sense of purpose often feels lost, easily influenced by others, and lacks the confidence to stand his ground. A solid masculine frame comes from understanding one's goals, values, and vision for the future. This sense of purpose drives every decision and action. When a man knows exactly what he stands for and where he's headed, he moves through life with direction and commitment. Purpose gives him the strength to overcome challenges, the focus to stay on track, and the clarity to prioritize what matters most. Without purpose, a man is prone to distractions and self-doubt, but with it, he becomes steady and unwavering.

Building and maintaining a masculine frame also involves knowing how to set healthy boundaries. Boundaries are about saying "yes" to yourself. A man with a strong frame understands his limits and is unapologetic about protecting his time, energy, and emotional well-being. He knows when to speak up for his needs and when to walk away from toxic relationships or situations that drain him. Boundaries show self-respect, and a man who values himself and his time is far less likely to be manipulated or taken advantage of. Setting clear, healthy boundaries also helps a man form deeper, more respectful relationships. He no longer looks for approval from others or tries to please everyone. Instead, he stays true to his own values and needs, maintaining his integrity.

A big part of having a strong masculine frame is the ability to lead, both in your own life and within your community. Leadership means inspiring others through your actions, showing strength, and building trust. A man with a solid masculine frame need not push his power onto others because his presence alone commands respect. He influences, motivates, and supports those around him. Leadership can look different in many situations, whether it's guiding a family with wisdom and protection, mentoring colleagues, or leading a community project. Leadership revolves around responsibility, and a man with a strong masculine frame understands that real power comes from accountability and service. He leads not out of ego, but because he is dedicated to helping others, knowing that his actions speak to his values and character.

Maintaining a strong masculine frame also means always striving for growth and self-improvement. A man who becomes stagnant or stuck risks losing his sense of direction and the strength that comes from developing his mind and body. Part of having a solid masculine frame is the discipline to keep evolving, whether it's taking on new challenges, learning new skills, or looking at things from different angles. Personal development is an ongoing journey. Whether it's reading, networking, traveling, or picking up new hobbies, a man must keep pushing himself out of his comfort zone. Doing this helps him stay adaptable and resilient, able to handle whatever life throws at him without losing sight of who he is.

Self-reflection is essential to maintaining a masculine frame. A man dedicated to personal growth should regularly check in with himself on his thoughts, actions, and reactions. This helps him stay aligned with his values and purpose, making sure he doesn't stray from his path. It also lets him see his weaknesses, improve himself, and adjust when needed. A man who reflects often can notice when he's acting out of line with his masculine frame and correct course before negative patterns take hold.

Amid distractions and pressures, building and maintaining a masculine frame is a lifelong journey that requires constant effort, discipline, and commitment. It's a process that involves physical strength, emotional control, clear purpose, healthy boundaries, and leadership. A man with a strong masculine frame lives with confidence and becomes a source of strength and inspiration for others. His presence is powerful, his actions intentional, and his leadership grounded in integrity. In the end, maintaining a masculine frame is about growing the strength, clarity, and wisdom to live with purpose and impact. Through consistent effort, self-reflection, and discipline, any man can build and sustain a masculine frame that allows him to thrive and lead in a constantly changing world.

CHAPTER 5

Live Below Your Means

"Financial freedom provides a peace of mind."

Where success is often measured by material possessions and outward signs of wealth, living below your means might seem strange or even unpopular. But living below your means is one of the most effective ways to achieve financial freedom, personal security, and lasting happiness. It's a lifestyle focused on thoughtful spending, making mindful decisions, and developing financial discipline. In a world filled with consumerism and constant advertising, choosing simplicity and putting long-term financial well-being ahead of instant gratification is both a smart and bold move. This chapter will explore the principles and benefits of living below your means, helping you break free from the cycle of debt and overconsumption while finding more peace and satisfaction in life.

Living below your means is about aligning how you spend with what matters to you and your long-term goals, instead of being driven by what society expects or chasing after temporary desires. It's a choice to prioritize financial stability and emotional well-being over the fleeting joy of owning more things. This mindset shift moves away from a culture of instant gratification and embraces a lifestyle built on delayed rewards and sustainability. For many, this change starts with realizing that happiness isn't found in accumulating more stuff, but in living within your means, investing in meaningful experiences, and creating a strong foundation for the future. When you focus on what really matters like health, relationships, growth, and peace of mind, you start to build a life full of rich experiences, not just possessions.

The first step in living below your means is understanding exactly where your money is going. A lot of people live paycheck to paycheck without ever fully realizing how much they're spending. To escape this cycle, you need to track your expenses carefully. This involves spotting areas where you may be overspending or living beyond your means. Start by creating a budget, tracking your income and expenses, and breaking them down into categories. Whether you use an app, a spreadsheet, or just good old pen and paper, keeping track of your finances can really open your eyes. It helps you see where you might be wasting money on things you don't need, like subscriptions, dining out, or random impulse buys. Once you have a clear picture of where your money is going, you can start making smarter choices about how to manage it.

Living below your means isn't cutting yourself off from everything but being more mindful of your priorities. It's about shifting from the "keeping up with the Joneses" mindset to focusing on what matters to you, instead of chasing after temporary wants pushed by consumer culture. One of the first places to start is with housing. Rather than stretching your budget to afford a big house, think about downsizing to a smaller, more affordable space, or finding a living situation that better matches your financial goals. Housing often takes up the largest part of a person's budget, so being thoughtful about where and how you live can really improve your financial health. A smaller home or a modest apartment can offer just as much comfort, and the money you save can go towards building your savings, making investments, or paying off debt.

A big part of living below your means is minimizing debt. Debt, especially high-interest debt like credit cards, can seriously hold you back from achieving financial freedom. It pulls you down and keeps you from living within your means. To live below your means, you need to shift your mindset and actively work on paying off any existing debt as quickly as possible. It might take some sacrifices in the short term, but the long-term rewards are worth it. Once you're free from the weight of debt, you'll feel a sense of relief and peace of mind. Instead of stressing over bills, you can start focusing on building wealth and enjoying the things that really matter. Living below your means, means understanding that debt is a tool that should be used carefully, and when you can, it's better to avoid it in favor of saving up and paying for things upfront.

Living below your means involves adopting a mindful approach to spending. With advertising, social media, and endless consumer options constantly in our faces, it's easy to get caught up in impulse buying or emotional spending. To avoid this, practice being intentional when making purchases. Before buying something, ask yourself if it aligns with your values and if it will bring long-term happiness or fulfillment. Instead of buying just because something looks good or is "on sale," focus on things that actually improve your quality of life and contribute to your well-being. Often, the things that matter most aren't the stuff we buy, but the experiences we create and the relationships we build. Living below your means is about prioritizing long-term satisfaction over short-lived pleasures.

One of the best parts of living below your means is the freedom it brings. When you're no longer constantly struggling to cover your expenses, the weight of financial stress lifts. This freedom lets you make decisions based on what you value and want, instead of feeling trapped in a cycle of working endless hours just to keep up with the latest trends. Living within your means gives you the space to follow your passions, take risks, and enjoy life without always stressing about how to pay your bills or handle debt. It opens up the door to financial independence whether that's the ability to retire early, travel the world, or dive into a career you love without worrying about money.

Along with financial freedom, living below your means also brings a sense of security and peace of mind. Financial stress is a huge source of anxiety for many people today. When you live below your means and save regularly, you build a safety net for yourself. Emergency savings, investments, and thoughtful planning for the future provide the security you need to handle the unexpected, like job loss, health issues, or other surprises. This security is about more than having money; it's about the peace of mind that comes with knowing you're ready for whatever life throws your way.

Adopting the habit of spending less than you earn encourages personal growth. When you downsize your lifestyle, pay attention to your spending, and focus on what really matters, you develop discipline and resilience. Over time, you get more comfortable with delayed gratification and become less swayed by external pressures. This gives you a sense of empowerment as you take control of your finances and your decisions. You'll discover that material possessions or constant upgrades aren't necessary for feeling fulfilled. Instead, you'll find satisfaction in simplicity, financial stability, and living a life that reflects your values.

Ultimately, Spending less is about creating a sustainable, intentional lifestyle that brings long-term fulfillment and financial independence. It's about appreciating what you have rather than always chasing after more. It's about making thoughtful choices that bring lasting satisfaction, not short-lived happiness from buying things. When you spend less, you build financial security and gain the freedom to live life on your terms. You create the space to focus on what matters: your health, relationships, personal growth, and the pursuit of a meaningful, purpose-driven life.

CHAPTER 6

Social Life of Abundance

"Cultivate an abundant social life. Connect with positive people."

With technology keeping us connected more than ever, it's easy to forget just how important real, human connections are. Yet, having a social life filled with deep, meaningful relationships is still a big part of feeling fulfilled and well. The people we connect with influence our emotional health, give us a sense of belonging, and play a huge role in our personal growth. While social media might make us

43

feel connected, it's the face-to-face conversations, shared moments, and true emotional bonds that really add value to our lives. This chapter looks at how to build a rich social life by creating authentic relationships, engaging with others in meaningful ways, and surrounding yourself with friends, mentors, and loved ones who support and uplift you.

A fulfilling social life begins with being authentic. It's easy to fall into the trap of trying to be who we think others want us to be, especially when we're in social situations. But real connection only happens when we show up as our true selves. Authenticity is about being honest with yourself and others about your values, interests, and emotions, and expressing them without holding back. It's about being vulnerable in your interactions and letting people see the real you, without worrying about judgment or rejection. When you approach social situations this way, you create space for others to do the same, and that's when trust, openness, and deeper connections can grow.

Authenticity is what turns casual interactions into genuine friendships.

Building an abundant social life takes effort. It's easy to get lost in the hustle of work, family responsibilities, and personal goals, leaving social connections at the bottom of the to-do list. But building and maintaining meaningful relationships requires time, intention, and consistency. A rich social life requires making room for others, reaching out, and staying open to new opportunities. One way to make this happen is to stay engaged with your social circle. Whether it's sending a thoughtful message, planning regular catch-ups, or inviting friends to hang out, the key is to put time and effort into your relationships and let them grow over time.

Genuine connections are formed through shared experiences, so the more effort you put in, the more you'll get out of it. Another important part of having an abundant social life is surrounding yourself with people who lift you up and inspire you. While it's good to have connections with a variety of people, the quality of those relationships is far more important than the number of them. Spend your time with individuals who align with your values, who push you to grow, and who support your goals.

Positive social interactions can greatly affect your mindset and emotional health. When you surround yourself with people who encourage your growth and celebrate your wins, you create an atmosphere of mutual respect and happiness. On the other hand, toxic or draining relationships can hold you back and lower your sense of self-worth.

An abundant social life is all about spending time with people who lift you up, not those who bring you down. While taking care of your existing friendships is important, it's just as important to grow your social circle if you want a fulfilling social life. To build a rich and diverse network, you need to step outside your comfort zone and be open to meeting new people. This might mean joining a club, attending social events, or taking part in activities that match your interests.

The best part about expanding your social circle is that it introduces you to fresh perspectives, new ideas, and opportunities for growth. You get the chance to connect with people from different backgrounds, learn from them, and discover what you have in common. Plus, the more you put yourself in different social situations, the better you get at relating to all kinds of personalities, making your social experiences even more rewarding.

Along with seeking out new connections, it's also important to develop the qualities that make you a good friend and social partner. Empathy, active listening, and kindness are all essential in building meaningful relationships. To create an abundant social life, you need to be fully present in your interactions. This means having conversations and also being genuinely engaged and interested in what others have to say.

Active listening is more than just hearing words; it's about understanding the emotions, needs, and viewpoints behind them. When people feel heard and understood, they're more likely to connect with you on a deeper level. Kindness and empathy also build trust, which makes it easier to form lasting relationships. One of the most rewarding aspects of a rich social life is the sense of community it creates.

Humans are naturally social creatures and having a group of people who share your interests, goals, and values can really boost your sense of belonging. A strong community supports you during tough times, celebrates your wins, and gives you stability and comfort. To build this sense of community, you need to be ready to give as much as you get. Be there for others when they need it, offer support and encouragement, and invest in the happiness and success of your friends and loved ones. When you contribute positively to your social circle, you strengthen those relationships and also create an environment where everyone feels encouraged to do the same.

A community built on mutual care and respect becomes an amazing source of strength and fulfillment. To create a rich social life, it's also important to find balance. While connecting with others matters, it's also essential to make time for self-care and personal space. The most fulfilling social lives are the ones where people can maintain a sense of independence and balance. Pushing yourself too much socially or sacrificing your well-being for others can lead to burnout and resentment. To avoid this, make time for activities that recharge you, whether it's enjoying a personal hobby, spending time alone, or setting boundaries to protect your energy. Keeping this balance allows you to show up as your best self in your social interactions and stay present in ways that work for you.

An abundant social life also means being willing to embrace vulnerability. Opening up and sharing your true thoughts, feelings, and experiences with others helps create a more genuine connection. Vulnerability lets people connect with you on a human level and builds trust. While it can feel uncomfortable sometimes, it's sometimes in those moments of honesty and openness that the strongest bonds are formed. Vulnerability helps you build empathy, break down barriers, and connect with others in a more meaningful way. When you're open and transparent, it encourages others to do the same, creating a space where emotional intimacy and real connection can grow.

Finally, a rich social life should bring joy and fulfillment, not stress or a sense of obligation. When your relationships are based on authenticity, respect, and shared values, they naturally become a source of happiness and enrichment. Instead of seeing socializing as just another task to check off your list, a fulfilling social life lets you enjoy the simple pleasures of companionship, laughter, and shared memories. It's about quality over quantity, building a few deep, meaningful connections rather than collecting a long list of acquaintances. When you focus on meaningful relationships, your social life becomes a source of lasting joy and satisfaction.

In conclusion, an abundant social life is about more than having a bunch of shallow connections or chasing validation. It's about building strong, meaningful relationships that add value to your life, push you to grow, and create a sense of brotherhood and loyalty. Being authentic, proactive, and empathetic while surrounding yourself with people who support and challenge you helps you create a circle that elevates you. With the right intention, effort, and a willingness to open up to others, you'll craft a social life that's not just about having a full schedule but about having real, powerful connections that push you to be the best version of yourself. The right circle supports you and fuels your ambition, helping you level up in every area of life.

CHAPTER 7

Life Insurance

"Leave your children or family money behind. When you die you can't take it with you. Write a will. This is a start to creating generational wealth."

Life insurance is one of those things people often push to the side, thinking it's something they do not need until it becomes a problem. But for men, making sure life insurance is in place is one of the smartest decisions they can make. It provides peace of mind, protects loved ones, and makes sure that if something unexpected happens, their family will not be left struggling.

This chapter explores why life insurance matters for men at different stages of life. One of the biggest reasons to have it is to provide financial security for family. Whether you are married, have kids, or are raising a child on your own, life insurance makes sure your loved ones are taken care of if something happens to you. It can help cover funeral costs, pay off outstanding debts, and, most importantly, give your family the ability to maintain their lifestyle without added financial stress.

Think about what happens when a family loses its main provider. Without life insurance, a spouse and children could struggle just to cover daily expenses. Life insurance acts as a safety net, replacing lost income and giving the family room to grieve without the added pressure of financial survival. Men, especially in their 30s to 50s, tend to carry significant financial responsibilities. Mortgages, car loans, credit card debt, and student loans are just some of the obligations that add up over time. If something were to happen to you, who would be left to handle those payments? Without life insurance, your loved ones could find themselves buried under financial stress with no clear way out.

Life insurance takes that burden off their shoulders, covering debts so your family isn't left scrambling to make ends meet. Having coverage means you can have peace of mind knowing that your financial responsibilities will be handled and that your family won't be put in a difficult position. For many men, a home is their biggest asset. Mortgages often stretch over decades, and if the primary earner is no longer around, keeping up with payments could become nearly impossible. Life insurance provides a safety net that helps pay off the mortgage, allowing your family to stay in the home they've built and worked so hard to maintain.

In addition to covering the mortgage, life insurance can help with maintenance and other property-related expenses, keeping the home a stable and secure place for your family even when you are no longer around. For men who own a business, life insurance is an important tool for protecting both the company and the people who rely on it. If something happens to you, it can provide the funds needed to keep things running smoothly, whether that means buying out your share, paying off business debts, or making sure there is a clear succession plan in place.

It also helps prevent business partners or family members from dealing with unnecessary financial stress during an already difficult time. Without the right coverage, the future of your business could be at risk. While life insurance is mainly about protection, it can also play a role in a broader financial strategy. Some policies, like whole life or universal life insurance, build cash value over time, which can be used as extra savings for retirement. These options offer flexibility and a way to grow wealth while giving you peace of mind, knowing your family is financially secure. For men looking to build long-term savings or leave a financial legacy, life insurance can be a valuable asset in planning for the future.

Many men want to leave something behind for their children or loved ones, and life insurance is a great way to make that happen. It provides financial security and allows you to build a legacy. Whether that means helping with your children's education, supporting a cause you care about, or making sure your family has a financial cushion, life insurance makes it possible. One of its biggest advantages is how it lets you pass on wealth in a direct, reliable way without complicated tax issues. It is a simple and effective way to leave a lasting impact on your family and future generations.

Waiting too long to get life insurance can be a mistake. The younger and healthier you are when you buy a policy, the more affordable it will be. A lot of men assume they will not need it until they are older, but life is unpredictable. Having coverage in place, no matter your age or health, gives you peace of mind knowing your loved ones will be taken care of if anything happens to you.

Life insurance is a financial decision, but it is also an emotional one. It shows your family that you have considered their future, that you care, and that you are prepared for the unexpected. Whether you are just starting a family, building your career, or approaching retirement, having life insurance is an investment in your peace of mind and the well-being of the people who matter most to you.

CHAPTER 8

Investing

"You must invest, or you will retire broke. The sooner you start the better. Compound interest is the key to creating wealth."

Before getting into the benefits of investing in index funds, it helps to first understand what they are. An index fund is a type of mutual fund or exchange-traded fund (ETF) designed to follow the performance of a specific market index. An index is simply a group of stocks, bonds, or other securities that represent a portion of the financial markets. For example, the S&P 500 tracks the 500 largest publicly traded companies in the U.S. When you invest in an index fund that follows the S&P 500, you're buying a small piece of all 500 companies in that index. Instead of picking individual stocks, an index fund gives you a diversified portfolio automatically. The goal is to match the market's performance rather than beat it, and historically, the market has delivered strong and steady returns over time.

One of the biggest advantages of index funds is that they cost far less than actively managed funds. Actively managed funds rely on professional fund managers to research, pick stocks, and make frequent trades, which leads to higher fees, often referred to as the expense ratio. On the other hand, index funds are passively managed, meaning they simply track an index without the need for constant oversight. This keeps fees significantly lower, sometimes just a fraction of what you'd pay for an actively managed fund. Lower fees mean more of your money stays invested and working for you instead of being eaten up by management costs. Over time, those savings add up. Even cutting fees by just 1% per year could mean thousands of extra dollars in your pocket over several decades, making a huge difference in your overall investment returns.

Investing in individual stocks can be pretty risky. If just one of the stocks you own takes a dive, your whole investment portfolio could take a hit. However, with an index fund, your money is spread across many different stocks, which reduces the risk of taking a big loss from any one company's downturn. For instance, if you invest in an index fund that tracks the S&P 500, you're putting your money into 500 different companies, from tech giants like Apple and Microsoft to consumer staples like Coca-Cola and Procter & Gamble. If one sector or a few companies struggle, your entire index fund won't feel the impact as sharply as it would if you were all-in on a single stock. Diversification is a crucial strategy for managing risk and aiming for steady, long-term gains. It's a fundamental investing principle and one reason why index funds are a favorite among seasoned investors.

Another big plus for index funds is their consistency. Sure, the stock market has its ups and downs in the short term, but over the long haul, it generally trends upwards. Putting your money in an index fund means you are part of the overall market's growth over time. Reacting to daily market fluctuations might be tempting, but research consistently shows that long-term investments in index funds usually outperform attempts at timing the market or picking individual stocks. Even during significant market downturns like the 2008 financial crisis or the COVID-19 market crash, the market eventually bounced back and continued to grow. Those who maintained their investments in index funds through those rough patches experienced significant benefits. Since index funds mirror the broader market, they provide steady returns that track the overall economic health. Over the years, the U.S. stock market has averaged about a

7% return annually after inflation. Despite the short-term swings, the longer-term trend has been positive, making index funds a solid choice for building wealth over time.

For many people, the charm of index funds is all about simplicity. Unlike actively managed funds, which need frequent trading and close attention, index funds are a "set it and forget it" investment. Once you put your money into an index fund, you don't have to stress over daily decisions or dig into the details of individual companies. This laid-back approach is especially attractive for busy professionals, those new to investing, or anyone who prefers not to get tangled in the intricacies of stock picking. With index funds, you can kick back and focus on other areas of your life, comfortable in the knowledge that your investment is ticking along with minimal fuss on your end.

One of the biggest perks of investing in index funds is tapping into the power of compound interest.

Compound interest means you earn interest on your initial investment and any accumulated interest from previous periods. Over time, this can lead to impressive growth in your wealth. For instance, imagine you invest $5,000 in an index fund with an annual return of 7%. After the first year, you're looking at $5,350. The next year, you're earning 7% on $5,350, not just the original $5,000. This compounding effect keeps rolling, and the longer your money stays in the fund, the more it grows. Starting early can really maximize these benefits. With their consistent returns and low fees, index funds are a solid choice for long-term investors aiming to make the most out of compound interest.

Index funds have become hugely popular because they're incredibly accessible to pretty much everyone. You don't have to be a financial guru or have heaps of money to start investing in them. Many brokers and retirement plans offer low minimum investments, which means you can start small and gradually boost your investments as you go. Plus, you can invest in index funds through tax-advantaged accounts like IRAs and 401(k)s, which helps you grow your wealth more efficiently by taking advantage of tax-deferred or, in some cases, tax-free growth.

Investing in index funds is a straightforward, effective, and cost-efficient strategy for building wealth over time. Whether you're just starting out in investing or you're looking to add a reliable element to your current portfolio, index funds are a great choice. They offer a simple, diversified, and consistent way to put your money in the markets, aiming for solid returns while keeping risks and fees low. With a long-term perspective and the power of compound interest, index funds can help you meet various financial goals, be it saving for retirement, purchasing a home, or just building up your savings for the future.

Investing in index funds allows you to focus on the things that matter most in life, knowing that your money is working for you, steadily growing with minimal effort. It's a smart, stress-free way to secure your financial future.

Chapter 9

Self-Grooming

"Perception is reality. Always look presentable. Self-care is key to confidence"

Self-grooming involves looking good, feeling confident, taking care of yourself, and showing respect for those around you. For many men, grooming might seem optional or superficial. Yet, it plays a significant role in both personal and professional life. It's a fundamental part of self-care that affects how you see yourself, how others perceive you, and even your success in life.

In this chapter, we'll explore why self-grooming is important for men, serving as a tool for personal growth, boosting confidence, and making a positive impression. Whether you're preparing for a big meeting, a night out, or just aiming to take better care of yourself, mastering self-grooming is a powerful way to show the world the best version of yourself.

The old saying "You never get a second chance to make a first impression" really does ring true in many situations, and grooming is one of the first things people notice. Whether you're heading to a job interview, out on a date, or just hanging out at a casual social event, how you look plays a big role in how others see you. Clean, neat grooming shows that you're responsible, pay attention to details, and have self-respect. Studies have found that people who keep themselves well-groomed are generally seen as more competent, confident, and professional. Conversely, poor grooming might lead others to form inaccurate opinions about you. No matter the setting, whether formal or laid-back, the way you present yourself can really influence how you're treated and the doors that may open for you.

But it's not all about the external perceptions, self-grooming is also a powerful way to boost your own confidence. Taking the time to look after yourself sends a positive message to your subconscious that you're worth the effort. This bit of self-care can really enhance how you feel about yourself, uplifting your mindset and overall emotional well-being. Think about the boost you get from a fresh haircut or wearing a well-fitted suit. Simple grooming habits can make you feel more together and prepared to face whatever comes your way. When you look good, you tend to feel better about yourself, and that newfound confidence shows in how you interact with others. It helps you handle tough situations with grace, whether you're socializing, at work, or dealing with personal matters.

Grooming involves maintaining your health and hygiene. Regular grooming keeps your body clean, odor-free, and reduces the risk of skin problems like ingrown hairs or acne. Keeping up with haircuts and beard trims helps you look sharp and prevents your hair from becoming tangled or unruly. Maintaining good oral hygiene with regular brushing and flossing helps ward off dental issues and keeps your breath fresh. Grooming is a practical approach to taking care of your body. Dedicating a bit of time to personal grooming helps you stay healthy, comfortable, and confident every day.

Self-grooming also reflects a form of self-respect and respect for the people you meet. When you take the time to groom, you're telling the world, "I value myself, my appearance, and my well-being." It's an act of self-love that highlights the importance of taking care of yourself in all aspects.

Taking care of yourself builds self-respect, which affects how you interact with others. When you prioritize self-care, you feel more energetic, motivated, and focused. This helps you tackle personal and professional tasks and responsibilities. Grooming creates a routine that supports your overall well-being and keeps your mindset positive for success.

In a competitive world, how you present yourself matters for professional success. Your skills and qualifications are very important, but your appearance and grooming also impact how others see you at work. Whether you work in a corporate or casual environment, looking polished can change how your bosses, colleagues, and clients view you. People see a well-groomed individual as organized, dedicated, and capable. Attention to detail matters in business, and caring for your appearance shows that you value your work and how others see you. Simple grooming habits, such as keeping facial hair trimmed, having clean nails, or wearing well-fitting clothes, can improve your professional image.

Grooming is important for attracting the right attention in social situations, like dating, socializing, or networking. When you take the time to groom yourself, it shows that you value yourself and care about your interactions. People are drawn to those who look well-groomed, as it reflects confidence, self-discipline, and an awareness of social norms. In dating, how you present yourself can significantly impact how others see you. A clean shave or well-kept beard, fresh clothes, and a neat appearance can be just as important as being friendly and engaging. Good grooming boosts your confidence when meeting new people and helps you make a positive first impression.

Grooming also lets you express your personal style. Your choice of clothes, hairstyle, and facial hair reflects who you are. Are you classic and sophisticated, modern and edgy, or relaxed and casual? Your grooming routine gives you a chance to show off your personality and create a look that feels true to you. Whether you like a clean-shaven look, a well-groomed beard, or a trendy hairstyle, grooming is a way to highlight your individual style. Putting effort into your appearance can help you feel more confident and ready to present the best version of yourself.

Self-grooming is about more than looking good. It involves taking care of your body and showing respect for yourself and others. It can boost your confidence and help you succeed in various areas of life. Whether you're seeking a promotion, trying to impress someone on a date, or just want to feel comfortable in your own skin, grooming plays an important role.

When you take care of your appearance, it can create a positive cycle. You feel more confident, people see you in a better light, and you can tackle challenges with a more positive attitude. Grooming is a powerful tool that can help you achieve success, maintain well-being, and present the best version of yourself.

CHAPTER 10

Saving

"You need an emergency fund of three to six months of living expenses.
Save this money fast as possible"

Saving money is one of the most valuable skills you can learn in life. In our busy lives, it's easy to forget how important it is to put aside money for the future. Whether you want to buy a home, prepare for retirement, or keep financial safety for you and your loved ones, saving is essential to your personal financial health.

For men, saving is a financial plan; it is a way to take charge of your future and safeguard what matters most. In this chapter, we will look at why saving is so valuable for both your peace of mind and the opportunities it can provide in your life.

One of the main reasons to save money is to protect your financial security. Life can be unpredictable, and emergencies can arise at any time. Whether it's losing a job, facing medical bills, or dealing with an unexpected home repair, having savings helps shield you from these surprises. Without savings, these sudden costs can lead you into debt or force you to rely on credit.

When you save money, you create a safety net that gives you peace of mind. You won't have to worry constantly about what could go wrong. Instead, you can focus on your life, knowing you have a backup if things get tough. This security is especially important if you support a partner or children, as it makes sure that your loved ones are cared for if something happens to you.

Saving money can help you create wealth. It regularly allows you to build up money to invest in things like real estate, stocks, or retirement accounts. The sooner you start saving, the more you can benefit from compound interest, which helps your money grow over time.

Think of saving as the first step in your journey to wealth. Without savings, you won't have the funds to invest and generate passive income for financial freedom. Every dollar you save today helps you build a better future. Saving gives you the chance to avoid living paycheck to paycheck and allows you to make choices that support your long-term goals.

Retirement may seem far away if you're in your twenties or thirties, but it's important to start saving as soon as you can. Even small amounts saved regularly can grow into a large sum over time because of compound growth. Relying only on Social Security or pensions can be risky, as they may not provide enough income to maintain your lifestyle.

Saving for retirement early helps you enjoy a comfortable future. Whether you use a 401(k), IRA, or another retirement account, setting aside money regularly helps make sure you're prepared when it's time to stop working. The earlier you start, the more your money can grow, allowing it to work for you even when you're not working.

Saving is important not just for a worry-free future, but also for achieving your personal goals. Everyone has dreams, whether it's buying a house, starting a business, traveling, or giving your children a great education. Without savings, these dreams can feel far away.

But when you save regularly and plan strategically, you can work toward achieving these milestones. It provides the freedom to pursue opportunities that match your values and desires. This might mean saving for a down payment on a home, starting an emergency fund for travel, or gathering the money to start your own business. No matter your goals, saving helps you move from just getting by to thriving and creating the life you want.

Debt is a major financial challenge for many men today. Whether it's from student loans, credit cards, or car loans, debt can make it hard to achieve your financial goals and take control of your money. Saving regularly helps you avoid relying on more debt for daily expenses or emergencies.

When you have savings, you're less likely to depend on high-interest loans or credit cards. The more you save, the more you can live within your means, and the less debt you'll build up. Financial independence starts with saving because it allows you to make purchases based on what you can afford instead of what you have to borrow.

Saving is also about showing younger generations the importance of saving. If you're a father or an uncle, teaching younger men about saving is one of the best ways to help them succeed. The habits you develop today are lessons they'll carry for life.

Teaching young people to save money early on helps them learn about financial independence, security, and planning for the future. You can show them how to grow their wealth, avoid debt, and take charge of their finances. Your actions today can lead to positive changes for years to come.

For many men, supporting their family is a top priority. Saving money keeps your family safe, no matter what happens. Whether you're creating a college fund for your kids or setting aside money to protect your spouse in case of an emergency, saving helps you care for the people you love.

Saving for your family's well-being is about meeting basic needs and giving them chances to succeed. Whether it's paying for extracurricular activities, helping with college costs, or ensuring stability during tough times, saving helps make sure your loved ones do not struggle financially due to unexpected events.

Saving money can feel overwhelming, especially if you're just starting out. But remember, saving is about being consistent. Even if you can only set aside a small amount each month, like $25 or $50, doing this regularly will help your savings grow over time.

The habit of saving helps you benefit from compound interest, which means your money can increase even faster as you save more. As you add more to your savings, you might be surprised at how quickly your finances improve. Keep in mind that wealth takes time to build; it comes from steady and disciplined saving.

Saving is vital for your financial future. It gives you security, helps you build wealth, and allows for a comfortable retirement. Saving also supports your personal and family goals. Whether you want financial independence, a secure future for your family, or to achieve your dreams, saving is the first step towards financial success.

Start saving as soon as you can. The earlier you begin, the better off you will be. Saving lets you take control of your future and face life's challenges with confidence. You will be prepared for anything that comes your way. So, start today, no matter how small the amount, and take the first step towards a more secure and fulfilling future.

www.ingramcontent.com/pod-product-compliance
Lightning Source LLC
Chambersburg PA
CBHW061709120626
46550CB00003B/1161